Taming Plastic

WITHDRAWN

STOP THE POLLUTION

Albert Bates

GroundSwell Books

SUMMERTOWN, TENNESSEE

Library of Congress Cataloging-in-Publication Data available upon request.

We chose to print this title on paper certified by The Forest Stewardship Council® (FSC®), a global, not-for-profit organization dedicated to the promotion of responsible forest management worldwide.

MIX
Paper from
responsible sources
FSC® C001701

Stock photography: 123 RF
Cover and interior design: John Wincek

Printed in Hong Kong

GroundSwell Books
an imprint of Book Publishing Company
PO Box 99
Summertown, TN 38483
888-260-8458
bookpubco.com

ISBN: 978-1-939053-24-4

25 24 23 22 21 20   1 2 3 4 5 6 7 8 9

CONTENTS

INTRODUCTION

Why did we develop plastics? For thousands of years we relied on products from stone, bone, wood, animal skins, shells, and plant fibers to make our tools, clothing, weapons, and modes of transportation. There was hardly any waste. Whatever material was used, it would eventually break down in the soil when we were done using it.

That was also a problem. These natural materials were relatively easy to chip, rip, or break, so products made from them had to be replaced regularly. For thousands of years, people dreamed of a product that would last forever and could be made in any shape or color. Enter plastics.

The word "plastic" comes from the Greek word *plassein*, which means "to mold or shape." Plastics are so versatile that they can be formed into anything from a car body to a small replacement valve for someone's heart. They can be spun into fibers for the clothes we wear, incorporated into the devices we use for entertainment, and shaped into the dishes we eat from.

But . . . that's also a problem. Plastic is everywhere. Take just one hour out of your day and observe how much plastic you encounter. Don't forget the polyester in your T-shirt or the nylon in your carpet. Does your house have vinyl siding? Reach for your TV, smartphone, or computer mouse—there's that plastic again. You're probably brushing your teeth with a plastic toothbrush and your hair with a plastic hairbrush.

Forty percent of the 450 million tons of plastic produced each year is designed to be discarded after a single use, usually within a few minutes after it's been bought. Consider the 1,200 billion plastic bottles Coca-Cola produces each year or the plastic wrappers on your candy bars. What about plastic straws, shopping bags, or packaging?

This is a serious problem that isn't going away soon. But many creative people all over the world are working on how to tame the amount of plastic that's already in circulation. Others are experimenting with how to create natural materials that have the same qualities as plastic but that will break down quickly and harmlessly. Let's take a look at what goes into making plastics and how they became a part of so many items in our daily lives.

Currently, half the plastics we use are thrown away after a single use. That includes 2.5 million plastic bottles and 2.9 million Styrofoam cups, disposed of just in the United States—every hour. Each year, enough plastics are thrown away to circle the world four times.

CHAPTER

Is Plastic Fantastic?

Billions of years ago, when small organisms died, they settled to the bottom of the ancient ocean that covered much of the earth at that time. Under the heat and pressure of layers of sediment on the ocean floor, along with the earth's shifting surface, the bodies of those organisms eventually transformed into fossil fuels: natural gas, petroleum, and coal.

The Hunt for Plastic Begins

Through the last half of the 1800s, a number of people experimented with combinations of plants and petroleum to make materials that would last longer than a natural product. For instance, cellulose, which makes up the cell walls of many plants, was very useful because it was incredibly flexible, but manufacturers were looking for something that would be more durable.

The first plastic was made from nitrocellulose, a plant material, and created by Alexander Parkes in 1862 for the Great London Exhibition. German chemists in 1897 made a milk-based plastic that is still produced today for buttons.

The first widely available modern plastic was made from nitrocellulose and camphor resin, a coal tar. An American inventor named John Wesley Hyatt won a prize offered by a manufacturer that was looking for a low-cost alternative to the ivory used to make billiard balls. Hyatt's celluloid won with a bang because occasionally, according to Mr. Hyatt, "the violent contact of the billiard balls would produce a mild explosion like a percussion gun-cap." (Nitrocellulose is explosive.)

WHAT IS A POLYMER?

Strictly speaking, a polymer is a complex molecule made up of many identical pieces. Polymers can be found in many different substances, from DNA to sugars, but generally you can think of natural polymers as the materials we use for buildings, such as wood and rubber, and for clothing, such as wool and silk. Plastic is the name we give to all the synthetic polymers that have been invented in the last century or so.

Bakelite Hits the Stage

In 1907, a chemist by the name of Leo Baekeland combined formaldehyde (a preservative that can cause serious burns as well as cancer) with phenol (which is derived from foul-smelling and

nasty coal tar) to make a plastic named after him. Bakelite could be molded into nearly anything, and the resulting products would last for a long time. Families gathered around Bakelite radios, drove cars with Bakelite accessories, and made calls with Bakelite telephones. They washed clothes in machines with Bakelite blades and styled their hair with Bakelite brushes and combs.

You can break a piece of Bakelite, but you can't make it into something else. It can't be composted, and it will never go away. This is why we can still find very old Bakelite phones, radios, and combs that look nearly brand new. At first, people thought it was good that plastic lasted so long. Bakelite replaced valuable rhinoceros horn, elephant tusk, and tortoiseshell, and it was both cheaper and tougher.

Once the manufacturers figured out how to inject liquid plastic into a mold, factory workers could make almost thirty times more of an item per hour than they previously were able

to. Plastic objects not only lasted longer than objects made of natural materials, but they also could be made more quickly and inexpensively than ever before.

PLASTICS FOREVER

All animal products break down over time and need to be replaced. In fact, nothing is permanent in nature. Everything turns into food for something else. Plants become food for animals, and animals die and decompose, creating food for plants. But the plastics that have been created over the last one hundred years have stopped that natural cycle in its tracks. Plastic lasts and lasts. Like plant or animal matter, it too may break down into smaller pieces (called microplastic), but there is almost nothing in nature that will eat those pieces.

The United States is home to less than 4 percent of the world's population, but it generates one-third of the world's waste. Although quantities vary among countries, about 10 percent of solid waste is plastic.

Know Your Plastic

There are three main types of plastics: (1) thermoplastics (plastics that soften and melt if they get hot enough—think plastic wrap), (2) elastomers (plastics that bend but won't melt), and (3) thermosets (plastics that won't bend or melt). Most types of plastic have long names that are difficult to pronounce or remember, so they're known by abbreviations. Here are a few of the more common ones.

PVC = *polyvinyl chloride*

PVC is used to make credit cards, plastic pipes, shower curtains, window frames, flooring, and squeeze bottles.

PS = *polystyrene*

PS is found in foam peanuts, plastic tableware, and disposable cups.

PP = *polypropylene*

PP is used in everything from bottle caps, drinking straws, and yogurt containers to appliances and car fenders.

PA = *nylon*

PA is found in fibers, toothbrush bristles, flexible tubing, and fishing line.

PC = *polycarbonate*

PC is used in compact discs, eyeglasses, traffic lights, and bulletproof glass.

PU = *polyurethane*

PU is used to make furniture padding and thermal insulation. It's also one of the components of spandex, a synthetic fiber that makes fabric stretch, and is currently the sixth or seventh most commonly used plastic.

PCE = *perchloroethylene or tetrachloroethylene*

PCE is the most popular solvent in conventional dry cleaning.

Several other types of plastics are well known by their common names. *Silicone* is a heat-resistant resin that's used mainly as a sealant but is also popular for use in high-temperature cooking utensils and as a base resin for industrial paints and epoxies. *Teflon* is found in heat-resistant, slippery coatings, such as nonstick surfaces for frying pans, plumber's tape, and water slides.

BEWARE OF TEFLON

There are many health hazards with all types of plastics, but one in particular you should know about (because it may be a danger to you every day) is Teflon, a common coating for nonstick pans. This coating begins to break down when it's heated to very high temperatures and releases toxic particles and gases (some of which cause cancer). Sometimes you can tell when this has happened because the surface is less smooth and the pan is more difficult to clean. The problem is, you can't tell while you're using the pan that the coating has deteriorated.

Any food that cooks quickly on low or medium heat and coats most of the pan's surface—such as scrambled eggs, pancakes, or warmed-up leftovers—will probably cool down the pan enough to prevent problems. But frying meat in a thin Teflon pan could create a dangerous situation.

Be cautious when cooking food in a Teflon pan, and follow these tips to stay safe:

- Never preheat the pan.
- Don't cook the food on high heat. Use only medium or low heat.
- Use your exhaust fan to ventilate the kitchen when you cook in a Teflon pan.
- Don't broil or sear meats in Teflon pans.
- Use a heavy nonstick pan. It will take longer to get hot than an inexpensive, lightweight pan.
- Avoid chipping or damaging the pan. Use wooden spoons to stir the food, and don't clean the pan with steel wool. If you must stack nonstick pans, put a clean dish towel or pieces of paper towel between them.
- If a nonstick pan becomes damaged, throw it out!

We're Drowning in All This!

Until recently, the world was big enough to store all our plastic trash. There was always somewhere we could think of as "away" to send the plastic we no longer wanted. But now, plastics of all sizes are reaching the most remote and deepest parts of the planet. Cities have been shipping their trash out to sea and just dumping it. The problem with doing this is that the number of people being born and consuming plastic keeps growing, but we'll never have more ocean than we have now. Can the ocean keep up?

In 2015, a group led by Jenna Jambeck, an environmental engineer at the University of Georgia, estimated that between five and thirteen million tons of plastic waste enter the ocean each year, a number she expects will double by 2025. Up to 80 percent or

The ocean will contain one ton of plastic for every three tons of fish by 2025. By 2050, it will contain more plastic than fish, by weight.

more of the waste that accumulates on land, shorelines, or the ocean's surface or seabed is plastic. The most common items are plastic bags, which are easily blown around by the wind, as well as discarded fishing equipment and food and beverage packaging.

Although we know more than ever before what types of plastic are being discarded, how much of it there is, and where it's ending up, we still don't know much about how long it will last in the environment and what effects it will have on plant and animal life. We do know that more than 70 percent of plastic entering the ocean ends up on the seafloor, thousands of meters below the surface. Over time, it breaks down into tiny particles. One-third of the fish caught in the North Atlantic have microplastic particles in their stomachs.

Eighty-eight to 95 percent of the plastic polluting the world's oceans pours in from just ten rivers— eight in Asia and two in Africa.

Thirty-eight million pieces of plastic trash litter the shores of Henderson Island, a remote, uninhabited island in the South Pacific. Scientists who surveyed the area believe the island is covered in more plastic trash than anywhere else on the globe.

Microplastic is even found in animals living on the ocean floor. We don't know to what extent these particles will cause harm, but we *do* know that we're making more plastic all the time, so eventually the number of these tiny plastic pieces will increase.

Why Can't We Just Recycle It All?

Leftover plastic scraps that come from manufacturers are easy to sort by type and quality, so it's not difficult for the same industries that produced them to reprocess, trade, and reuse them. But it's not possible or practical to recycle everything.

Roughly half the plastic collected by recycling programs can't be repurposed. Many items contain several different types of plastic, each needing separate processes to break them down. Also, the plastic in recycled waste might have been damaged by heat, light, outdoor weathering, or simply by being used.

Consumer plastic gets collected curbside or from bins. It has to be separated from paper, metals, and other mixed waste and then cleaned. Only about half the plastic gathered by recycling programs

makes its way from curbside collections to plastics recycling facilities—the rest is already too difficult to separate, handle, or clean. Of that, 70–90 percent ends up as reusable plastic. However, so many chemicals must be added in order to make new plastic that it will never be able to be recycled again.

Let me repeat this once more: recycling plants are making single-use plastics that are incapable of ever being recycled again.

We need to clear up the morass of labeling to make it less confusing for people who want to recycle.

Recycling Plastic Comes to a Halt

The recycling rate for all plastics in the United States is meager—about 10 percent. But for many years, most of that small amount was shipped halfway around the world to China, where it would be recycled. This worked fairly well as long as people carefully separated their plastic from other waste.

Then consumers grew lazy. Ordinary bottles, cans, and paper went into blue bins along with plastic and were transported to recycling facilities that accepted everything all mixed together. It was up to that facility to sort the recyclables and then sell them to China. But vastly more recycling and less careful sorting resulted in increasingly contaminated bales of plastic—with bits of paper and metal mixed in. Foil-lined drink cartons and pouches containing a combination of plastic and paper could be anywhere in those bales. Even a tiny bit of unwanted material meant that the whole bale would be marked "contaminated" and rejected by processing plants in China.

China had to bear the cost of cleaning up this waste. To avoid extra shipping, it started sending its officials to recycling centers in the United States to inspect bales of recycled material before they left the warehouses.

We now make over twenty-five times more plastic than was made in 1960. By 2050, we'll be making seventy-five times more plastic than was made in 1960.

In 2017, China shocked the world by saying it had had enough. It wanted no more of our garbage. It was losing money, losing its environment, and harming its people's health. China's president Xi Jinping let it be known that the country would no longer accept other countries' trash and would focus more on curbing its own pollution.

Commercial and municipal recyclers in the US, Canada, Ireland, Germany, and other exporting countries were left to deal with rapidly growing mountains of plastic. In 2018, the amount of plastic sent to China and Hong Kong fell by more than 90 percent, but scraps being sent to Thailand, Malaysia, and Vietnam grew incredibly. Then all those countries announced that they would join China's plastic ban. Vietnam immediately stopped issuing new permits for recyclers and allowed existing permits to expire. Malaysia immediately revoked the permits of all 114 plastics importers. After a pilot whale washed up dead on a Thai beach in June 2018 with seventeen plastic bags in its stomach, Thailand announced that it, too, would join the ban.

It's unclear what is currently happening to all of the material sent to recycling centers in the United States. Some may still find its way to reprocessing plants, but a majority of it may be incinerated with other waste or simply dumped into landfills. What *is* clear is that we have a big problem.

CONTAMINATED CLOTHING

Clothing made from synthetic fibers, including polyester, nylon, and acrylic, is very inexpensive to manufacture and very bad for people and other living things. Because of its low price tag, it's tempting to buy it, and retailers and manufacturers may offer little else but clothing made with synthetics. Eighty-three percent of drinking water samples from around the world are contaminated with plastic fibers. Much of the contamination of fresh and saltwater occurs when clothing made from synthetic fibers is worn and washed.

What about Plastic from Plants?

California recently announced that it is joining a handful of other large economies around the world with plans to begin curtailing fossil fuel production. The end of the age of oil is now upon us, and that will have an impact on all types of plastic made from fossil fuels.

An option is to create plastic from plant material, known as bioplastics. Bioplastics are inexpensive to make, durable, and lightweight, but often they create just as much of an environmental problem as plastics made from fossil fuels. While some bioplastics could be made from crop residues, such as stalks and leaves, large quantities of plant material would be needed to meet the world's demand for plastic. It would take a considerable amount of fertilizers and pesticides made from fossil fuels to grow enough plant material to make bioplastics, resulting in even more greenhouse gases, ozone depletion,

Ninety-nine percent of all plastic is produced from fossil fuels. The manufacturing of plastics has a very large negative effect on the climate.

and contamination of drinking water. Although the manufacturing of some bioplastics could reduce the use of fossil fuels, other bioplastics may require just as much as conventional plastic.

When we started to use corn to make ethanol fuel, that process created a corn shortage that increased the price of corn products used for food. The same thing might happen if we switch to plant material to make plastics. Even if only 10 percent of all plastics were starch-based and derived from food crops—such as corn, soybeans, or sugarcane—it could drive up food prices, making food less affordable for the poorest people. This will become an even more difficult challenge when climate change alters growing seasons and population growth increases the demand for food and the ground to grow it in.

An advantage of bioplastics is that some are biodegradable. They're made from plant or animal material and will break down into organic waste once they are discarded. For instance, Plastarch is a biodegradable and heat-resistant plastic made from cornstarch.

However, there's a problem when biodegradable plastic bags and cups get mixed into the recycling stream—they gum up the works. For this reason they require carefully controlled separation and composting, which take a lot of space, energy, and labor.

Even if waste-sourced bioplastics and recycled resins can replace plastics made from fossil fuels, we still face a toxic legacy. Can poisonous products released in the past be collected and reprocessed? Can they degrade quickly and efficiently enough to prevent catastrophic damage in the future?

We May Always Want Some Plastic

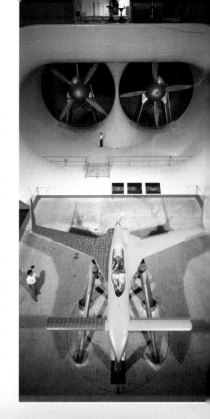

S ome uses for plastic are practical necessities, even when the plastic isn't recyclable, biosourced, or biodegradable. New types of plastics are allowing cars, planes, and trains to go farther using less fuel. Solar cells are being manufactured into thin films that can be painted on rooftops or layered onto clear glass windows. Plastic landfill liners, sewer pipes, flame-resistant electrical boxes and cables, and many other common items have been widely adopted for safety reasons.

You can complain about ziplock bags, but the truth is that they save a lot of food from spoiling, so they indirectly lower the cost of food. In city hospitals and rural clinics, medical plastics are the only materials sterile enough to rely on, precisely because microbes don't like them. And how many heart patients would want to have a biodegradable pacemaker in their chest?

This, then, must be our objective: we have to choose better plastics and reject worse ones.

Molding and Shaping a New Future

Now is not the best time to be dealing with our plastics problem. Fifty or one hundred years ago would have been better. Some of the problems caused by plastics can't be fixed now—they will be with us forever. But now is the second-best time to start, so let's go.

Although no solution is ideal, as was shown in the previous chapter, there are clear paths that each of us can explore. We can

- transform one type of plastic into another plastic or some other substance;
- make plastic into more efficient shapes;
- find sustainable ways to break down plastic; and
- create biodegradable bioplastics without burdening the world's food supply.

19

Shape-Shifting Plastic

Kathleen Draper, my coauthor of *Burn: Using Fire to Cool the Earth,* discovered by experimentation that there's a type of polystyrene (EPS) that dissolves quickly in acetone at room temperature. The lightweight, gummy product that's left can then be blended with up to 60 percent biochar (a type of charcoal) and molded into virtually any shape, which will harden in a few days. It could be shaped into roofing tile, surfboards, or outdoor furniture.

A number of companies are experimenting with how to convert one form of plastic into another. Recycling Technologies in Britain makes a machine that turns plastic waste into crude oil. MacRebur in Scotland is testing a recycled plastic road surface that is said to be stronger and more durable than asphalt roads and promises lower fuel consumption by reducing tire resistance on the road surface. Dell, the computer company, launched a pilot program in 2017 to recycle ocean plastics to make packaging trays for laptops. Adidas has begun making Ultraboost Uncaged Parley shoes from 100 percent recycled content.

Researchers at the University of Helsinki have been developing a way to recycle textiles, including polyester blends, using a nontoxic solvent called ionic liquid to dissolve old fabric into new. Ioncell can turn used textiles, pulp, or even old newspapers into new biodegradable fabrics without chemicals.

The organization Healthy Seas collects used and abandoned fishnets from the ocean and ships them to a factory in Slovenia that turns them into clothing. Aquafil, an Italian company sponsoring Healthy Sea's mission, turns these plastic nets into Econyl, a regenerated nylon fiber, by chemically dissolving them into oil, extruding it to a resin, and spinning that into high-quality, high-performance yarn that will become bikinis, leisure apparel, and athletic jerseys.

Rethinking Shape

Besides transforming the plastic we have, manufacturers are also looking into changing the actual shape of plastic packaging. There are good reasons why stand-up plastic pouches have come to replace so many aluminum cans, glass jars, and hard-plastic containers. They're lighter and use less material, saving energy and the costs of manufacturing and transportation. They're made by layering different kinds of plastics, each with unique advantages. An outer layer of polyester holds ink colors well and keeps oxygen out, so food stays fresher. A middle laminate of polyethylene keeps out moisture. An inner, metal-coated plastic layer keeps out light. And the packaging is rigid enough to stand up on a shelf, so the pouches can take up less space than jars or cans. The downside? Because they're made of layers of adhesive and different plastics with different melting temperatures, they're not recyclable. Moreover, in most recycling sorting facilities, flat objects, such as empty stand-up pouches, end up in the paper stream and get burned or landfilled.

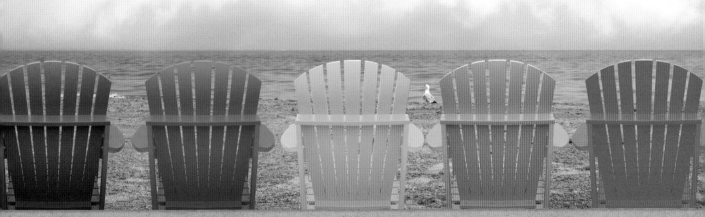

Because of that, Layfield Flexible Packaging, a Canadian company, has developed a special kind of plastic called BioFlex. Pouches made with BioFlex are designed to decompose in a landfill within ten years. Although they emit the dangerous greenhouse gas methane as they decay, these pouches are still more environmentally friendly than other kinds of packaging.

Chewing through the Plastic We Have

When a plant dies and drops to the ground, there is a progression of bacteria, fungi, worms, and microbes that work in combination or sequence to recycle nutrients, protective substances, and water to plants and create fresh soil. A similar type of decomposition might be used to break down plastics. Both petroleum-based and plant-based plastics can be biodegradable.

We need to find ways to biodegrade plastics in a relatively short time period—weeks or months—rather than the dozens or hundreds of years required for the fungi and bacteria naturally present in the environment to break down traditional plastics. Ideally the process should happen in nearly any natural environment or in a landfill, but in reality, it often requires controlled composting conditions for the proper mixture of air, heat, and microbes.

In 2016, Japanese scientists exploring an old waste dump discovered a microbe that had naturally evolved to eat plastic. After two years of laboratory work, an international team revealed the detailed structure of the enzyme produced by the microbe that did the work. In the process of tweaking the enzyme to see how it had evolved, they inadvertently made a new substance that was even better at breaking down the plastic in soft drink bottles than what was made by the parent microbe.

However, scientists may not have to discover the best microbes for decomposing plastics through time-consuming trial and error. It might be easier to simply "train" a particular fungus, for example, to consume food sources that it wouldn't previously have chosen. To do this, a polluting chemical might be introduced to a fungus in larger and larger quantities until the fungus learns to produce the right enzyme at the right amount to be able to survive and thrive in what were previously toxic conditions.

It may take several fungal specialists to break down some plastics, not just one. A 2018 study of all the microbes in the digestive system (known as the gut microbiome) of meal moths found that the worms could encourage the growth of whichever microbes were needed to consume completely different plastics.

Work in this area should proceed with caution. We should not even consider releasing a genetically modified plastic-eating microbe into the wild. The microbe that Japanese scientists found in a landfill had naturally evolved from bacteria that could slowly decompose cutin, a natural polymer that's a protective coating made by plants. Putting that process on steroids by tinkering with the genetic code of a natural organism could result in an evolutionary monster that could grow out of control. For instance, a genetically modified organism might not only eat plastics but also plants and animals.

Another approach would be to reengineer plastic to self-destruct. At the Center for Sustainable Polymers, scientists are designing plastic to dissolve when it encounters environmental triggers, such as light or seawater. One problem with this approach is that consumers may not like watching a milk container begin leaking all over the kitchen counter because someone spilled a bit of salt on a wet surface! But if plastic could be designed to automatically break down under the right circumstances, acres of landfill space could be saved.

LANDFILLS

For the plastics we can't refuse, reuse, recycle, keep using, break down, or compost, our best bet will be to collect and bury them in some well-designed sanitary landfill, either forever or until a better solution appears.

Landfills get a bad rap, and in many cases that reputation may be deserved if the landfills are poorly engineered, poorly managed, or leach or outgas poisons or greenhouse gases. But they still are going to have a role as we find ways to deal with our plastic mistakes of the past. Without landfills, the carbon that had been stored deep underground for millions of years as fossil carbon will, over the course of centuries, waft up from the earth's surface to the atmosphere and add to global warming.

Making Plastic from Renewable Resources

If there are limited options for creating new plastics from already-manufactured plastics or for decomposing existing plastic, would plastic from renewable resources, such as plants, be a good option? Experts say biobased plastics could eventually replace 90 percent of the traditional plastics we use.

Bioplastics have been made from food crops, including corn, wheat, sugarcane, potatoes, sugar beets, rice, and plant oil. (These are all crops that would have been used for human or animal food.) Other renewable resources are non-food crops (such as wood or waste materials from food crops). Ideally, bioplastics should come from non-food crops rather than compete with food crops and forests, as we discussed in the previous chapter.

Promising new source material for bioplastics may come from different types of algae. The big plus with algae is that they don't need fertilizers, pesticides, herbicides, or farmland to be produced. Some algal plastics biodegrade within twelve weeks in soil and five hours in water. Loliware, a company that appeared on the TV show *Shark Tank*, will replace many single-use plastics with bioplastic from kelp, which benefits ocean life and does not require fertilizer.

Starch is economical, abundant, and renewable and is the base material for about half of the bioplastics market. Starch-based plastic is so simple that it can be made at home; paper mâché is an example. Chemicals can be added to make these plastics more flexible and water resistant. Not all starch-based plastics are compostable, but they do have a lower carbon footprint than petroleum-based plastic.

Cellulose is the original natural plastic and is still the most abundant organic polymer on Earth. It's found in the cell walls of green plants and in many forms of algae. The cellulose content in cotton, wood, and hemp is particularly high. Cellulose can also be added to starch-based plastics to make them more water resistant.

Wheat gluten, soy protein, and casein (from milk) show promising properties as biodegradable polymers. Soy proteins have been used in plastic production for over one hundred years. Soy-based plastics are not as prevalent as fossil-based plastics because they absorb water and are expensive to use, but promising experiments are being done by adding soy to other plastics.

There's a whole world of new fabrics that are being developed from natural sources. These include sustainably harvested cork fabric as an alternative to leather; fish skin; mushroom "skin"

DIGGING A DEEPER HOLE

Every two decades, world plastic production doubles, and leading plastic manufacturers are planning to increase production by almost one-third over the next five years. Producers are taking the world in the wrong direction. A request to company executives and chemists: Please stop digging us into a deeper hole. To place the burden entirely on consumers, as most "solutions" do, is unfair. We should put pressure on the industries most responsible for plastic wastes and urge them to do a better job at handling, collecting, reusing, and disposing of plastic.

We also need new products designed to degrade under natural conditions. At a minimum, packaging materials (the largest stream of plastics) should break down into harmless components in saltwater. For products that need to function in marine environments, we might even consider replacing them with whatever was used *before* plastics, such as wood.

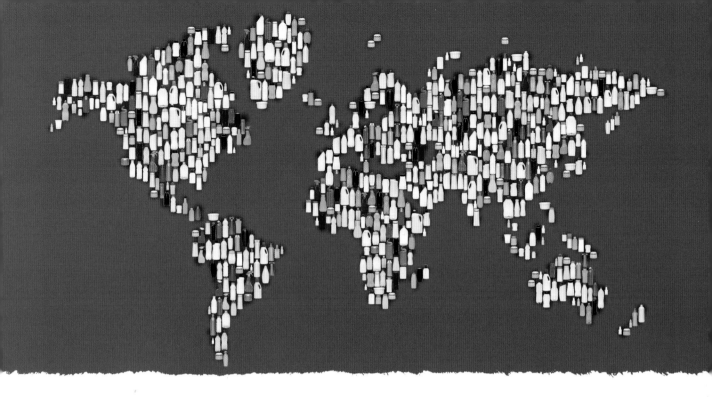

(the cap skin from a mushroom native to subtropical forests); pelle-mela, sustainably sourced from discarded apple peels and core waste from juiced apples; Piñatex from pineapple processing waste; Orange Fiber yarn and silks; TENCEL from beech and eucalyptus; and hemp, which is UV-, mold-, and mildew-resistant, naturally antimicrobial, absorbent, and durable.

BACK TO THE FUTURE

Is it possible that the plastics of the future will be made from materials designed to be naturally decomposed? In 1983, Marlborough Biopolymers developed a bacteria-based bioplastic called biopal. In the late 1990s, the Biotec company introduced its Bioflex, which is used in extruded films and molded plastics. Today those prod-ucts (or something very similar) are in sacks, bags, trash bags, diaper films, Bubble Wrap, protective clothing, gloves, labels, barrier ribbons, trays, flowerpots, freezer products and packaging, cups, pharmaceutical packaging, disposable cutlery, cans, containers, preformed pieces, CD trays, golf tees, toys, and writing materials.

4

Be an Emergency Planetary Technician

I am an EPT: emergency planetary technician. We've seen how plastics contribute to one of the planetary crises we now face. This chapter offers examples of emergency care that governments, companies, and you and I as individuals can provide. I believe that if many more people decide to join with me and become emergency planetary technicians, we have a decent chance of stabilizing the patient.

Government Taking the Lead

We don't have to wait for the United Nations or the US government to agree on how to tame plastics. Individual states and cities can take their own steps to create less plastic waste. In September 2018, California became the first US state to implement a partial ban on plastic straws. A few months later, Boston's plastic bag ban began for retail spaces of twenty thousand square feet or larger and will roll out to smaller businesses over the next few years.

STOP THE STRAWS!

If you're automatically given a plastic straw in a restaurant, return yours to your server and politely instruct them to

- provide a straw only when requested by a customer;
- provide either compostable or reusable straws; or
- get rid of straws completely.

An increasing number of countries have now imposed a ban on disposable plastics and plastic bags or have established targets for reducing plastic consumption and waste. Chile made history in 2018 when it became the first country in Latin America to ban the commercial use of plastic bags. After two of Australia's biggest supermarket chains announced that they would stop offering single-use plastic bags to their consumers, bag bans were enacted in all but one Australian state. By year's end, there had been an 80 percent drop in plastic bag consumption across the entire country.

Single-use plastics are also in the crosshairs. The Tamil Nadu government in India banned single-use plastic in the state starting in 2019. In 2018, the Parliament of the United Kingdom declared an initiative to cut back on single-use plastic wherever feasible or to replace it with more sustainable alternatives. As a result, the UK rolled out a range of new biobased, certified-compostable catering items, such as coffee cups, soup containers, and salad boxes, for use in the House of Commons and the House of Lords. The government plans to stop providing bottled water in Parliament, following the example of Buckingham Palace. New waste bins will be installed in Parliament and the royal palaces to capture used compostable items, and an organic recycling facility has agreed to make Her Majesty's compost.

The plastics problem is really a global one, so our focus should be on global solutions. Right now the regulation of plastics, including dumping into rivers, lakes, and the ocean, is left to decisions made in more than two hundred countries. Various groups and organizations are making an effort to create an updated and effective law of the oceans, but progress has been slow and has relied too much on voluntary commitments from industries and individuals. Stronger leadership is needed to address the problem sooner rather than later.

Companies in Action

Since 2002, Reet Aus, a clothing designer from the country of Estonia, has been upcycling—turning unwanted materials into new, mass-produced garments. For instance, her business partners in Bangladesh sweep up bits of unused fabric in factories that make clothing for popular brands, including Tommy Hilfiger and Calvin Klein.

Her collection, including a treasured shirt of mine, is entirely from post-production leftovers. She keeps proving that clever design can salvage mountains of wasted textiles and the labor and natural resources spent to produce them. Each garment in her clothing line will save on average 75 percent in water and 88 percent in energy. She also improves the working conditions of the shops she helps in Bangladesh.

The Danish toy maker Lego began selling new eco-friendly elements made out of sugar-based polyethylene that will be shaped like trees and plants. This new material is not strong enough to make regular Lego bricks, so the company is investing the equivalent of 150 million US dollars to find a way to make all of their Legos using biodegradable materials. Lego also committed to rely on 100 percent renewable energy by 2020 and to implement carbon-neutral manufacturing and raw materials at its plants. It is promoting recycling by encouraging families to recycle or donate unwanted Lego bricks.

Treating Plastic Like Currency

Some companies are approaching the recycling process in a very unique way. David Katz founded the world's largest chain of stores taking only used plastic as payment. Everything in the store, including school tuition, medical insurance, Wi-Fi, cell phone minutes, power, cooking fuel, and high-efficiency stoves, is purchased using plastic garbage. The stores are called the Plastic Bank. Any customer has the opportunity to earn a living by collecting material door-to-door, from the streets, or from business to business and taking it to the Plastic Bank, where it is weighed, checked for quality, and credited to the customer's online account, secure against robbery.

The Plastic Bank removes labels, caps, and grime and then either shreds the plastic and packs it into bales for export or recovers reusable bottles and other parts for reuse. For instance, Henkel, a personal-care products company based in Germany, is about to introduce shampoo in 100 percent recycled plastic bottles; half the plastic in those bottles will be "social plastic" from the Plastic Bank. Marks & Spencer, the large retailer in Great Britain, is making plastic shopping bags with the Plastic Bank's social plastic. The Plastic Bank currently operates in Haiti and the Philippines, with plans to expand into Brazil, India, and Ethiopia.

The Ocean Cleanup

The Great Pacific Garbage Patch is an area between Hawaii and California that contains the largest accumulation of ocean plastic in the world. In September 2018, a giant floating trash collector, The Ocean Cleanup, departed Alameda Works Shipyard in California bound for the Garbage Patch. Once the trash collector trapped a sufficient volume of plastic, the plan was for a service vessel to arrive to collect it with a drawnet and haul the net with a crane. The plastic would then be sorted and packed for delivery to recycling plants ashore.

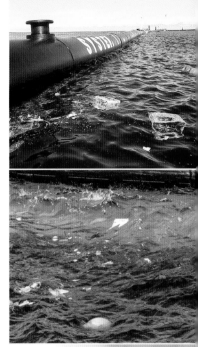

The Ocean Cleanup is the creation of Boyan Slat, a twenty-four-year-old Dutch entrepreneur. After a holiday diving trip in Greece, he got a sense of how much plastic trash is in the ocean, so he quit his aerospace engineering studies and made The Ocean Cleanup his life's mission. With the success of an initial crowdsourcing campaign, he was able to attract a top-notch staff of sixty-five dedicated engineers and scientists, many with years of experience designing platforms for oil companies.

Some critics say the project diverts attention away from what is regarded as a more cost-effective and efficient way to save the ocean—by preventing plastic trash from flowing into it in the first place. Although Slat recognizes that floating plastic accounts for only a fraction of the plastic that enters the ocean, he feels that several different simultaneous approaches to cleanup are not only possible but necessary. Marine experts were also concerned that the float might trap fish or mammals, but this hasn't turned out to be the case.

In addition to its effectiveness, The Ocean Cleanup was created with other benefits in mind. For the most part, it operates on its own, driven by ocean currents and wind. It can be made larger or smaller, depending on the need.

Rotterdam, Netherlands, could become the first city to pave its streets, highways, and bike paths with plastic collected by The Ocean Cleanup. It's experimenting with Lego-like paving blocks to replace fossil-sourced asphalt and concrete.

Slat hopes that by 2020, sixty additional systems will be at sea to gather more than fifteen thousand tons of plastic a year. The design is being changed and improved based on what was learned from the performance of the first system. The Ocean Cleanup estimates that with these simple systems, it can remove 50 percent of the Great Pacific Garbage Patch within five years and 90 percent of all ocean plastic by 2040.

Act with Conscience

What can you do? Do without. Start rejecting plastic in your life by simply refusing to be served a single-use plastic straw. Only buy wooden toys and home furnishings. Bag groceries in reusable cloth or, if you must, in paper. Buy biodegradables. If there is to be a future, this is where it begins.

Besides buying fabrics that last longer and can be recycled, purchase clothing made from organically produced materials that naturally biodegrade, such as cotton, silk, linen, and wool. Wash them only when they absolutely require it, especially outerwear. Be aware not to purchase blends. Many fabrics can be recycled, even acrylics, but if the process requires the entire structure to be disassembled, thread by thread, remanufacturers may shy away.

LIVING PLASTIC-FREE

In *Zero Waste: 50 Tips for a Plastic-Free Life*, author Caroline Piech offers ways for everyone to change their habits immediately. Here are some of her recommendations that haven't already been mentioned:

- Support farmer's markets, which are a great way to buy fresh, local produce without plastic packaging and stickers.

- Purchase fresh eggs in cardboard boxes, not polystyrene.

- Stop using disposable coffee pods or capsules.

- Store leftover food in glass, tin, or steel containers rather than Tupperware or other plastic storage containers.

- Stay away from viscose, nylon, spandex, and polyester.

- Learn how to repair clothes instead of throwing them out.

- Store cosmetic products in glass, metal, wood, cardboard, or paper containers.

- Choose toilet paper that is not wrapped in plastic.

- Use wooden or paper matches or refillable metal lighters instead of plastic disposable lighters.

- Avoid chewing gum! Many popular chewing gum brands are overloaded with plastic, synthetic rubber, and artificial sweeteners.

- Acquire secondhand any plastic items that are absolutely necessary.

- Use washable makeup pads.

- Use natural wipes and scrubbers instead of plastic dusters and synthetic sponges.

- Replace plastic cutting boards, cutlery, dishes, strainers, and mixing bowls with natural materials, such as wood, metal, bamboo, or compressed cotton.

- Wash your laundry with homemade laundry soap.

- Never flush cat litter down the toilet.

Every act you take to support an alternative to plastic results in a healthier planet. Hopefully, you will be able to tell your grandchildren of a time when plastic trash was everywhere and was an enormous problem, one that your generation decided to solve, and did.

"We cannot solve our problems with the same thinking we used when we created them."

ALBERT EINSTEIN

INDEX

GROUNDSWELL BOOKS

SOLUTIONS FOR A SUSTAINABLE WORLD

For more books that inspire readers to create a healthy,
sustainable planet for future generations, visit
BookPubCo.com

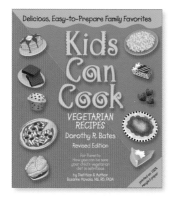

Kids Can Cook

Dorothy R. Bates
Suzanne Havala, MS,RD

978-1-57067-086-2 • $14.95

Vertical Gardening

A Complete Guide to Growing Food,
Herbs, and Flowers in Small Spaces

Jason Johns

978-1-57067-375-7 • $9.95

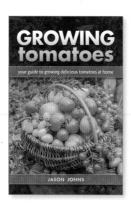

Growing Tomatoes

Your Guide to Growing
Delicious Tomatoes at Home

Jason Johns

978-1-57067-367-2 • $9.95

How To Start A Worm Bin

Your Guide to Getting Started
with Worm Composting

Henry Owen

978-1-57067-349-8 • $9.95

Purchase these titles from your favorite book source or buy them directly from:
Book Publishing Company • PO Box 99 • Summertown, TN 38483 • 1-888-260-8458
Free shipping and handling on all orders